D0463126

Osama bin Laden

The War on Terrorism

By Nancy Louis

NO LONGER PROPERTY
OF
SCAPPOOSE PUBLIC LIBRARY

War on
Terrorism

SCAPPOOSE PUBLIC LIBRARY
P.O. Box 400
SCAPPOOSE, OR 97056

Visit us at
www.abdopub.com

Published by ABDO Publishing Company, 4940 Viking Drive, Suite 622, Edina, Minnesota 55435. Copyright ©2002 by Abdo Consulting Group, Inc., Pentagon Tower, P.O. Box 36036, Minneapolis, Minnesota 55435 USA. International copyrights reserved in all countries. No part of this book may be reproduced in any form without written permission from the publisher.

Published 2002
Printed in the United States of America
Third printing 2003

Edited by Paul Joseph
Graphic Design: John Hamilton
Cover Design: Mighty Media
Illustrations: John Hamilton
Photos: AP/Photo, FBI

Library of Congress Cataloging-in-Publication Data

Louis, Nancy, 1952-
　　Osama Bin Laden / Nancy Louis.
　　　　p. cm. — (War on terrorism)
　　Includes index.
　　Summary: A biography of the Islamic extremist who uses his family wealth to fund and support worldwide terrorism and who has been linked to many terrorist attacks since the 1980s.
　　ISBN 1-57765-663-6
　　1. Bin Laden, Osama, 1957- 2. Terrorists—Biography—Juvenile literature.
3. Terrorism—Juvenile literature. [1. Bin Laden, Osama, 1957- 2. Terrorists 3. Terrorism]
I. Title. II. Series.

　　HV6430.B55 L68 2002
　　958.104'6'092—dc21
　　[B]

2001055220

Table of Contents

September 11, 2001

The South Tower of New York's World Trade Center collapses after being struck by a hijacked airliner. The North Tower, already in flames from an earlier terror attack, collapsed shortly afterward.

Day Of Terror

ON TUESDAY, SEPTEMBER 11, 2001, THE early morning weather along America's east coast was sunny and cool. It was a typical autumn day until the unthinkable happened.

American Airlines Flight 11 from Boston, Massachusetts, to Los Angeles, California began much like the other flights that take off each day. The Boeing 767 took off from Boston's Logan International Airport at 7:59 A.M. with 92 passengers and crew on board.

Less than an hour after Flight 11 took off, Michael Woodward, a ground manager at Logan, answered his phone to find Madeline Sweeney, a flight attendant, on the other end. She was calling from the airplane of Flight 11. "This plane has been hijacked," she told him. She went on to say that the hijackers had stabbed two flight attendants. She also said it appeared the hijackers had killed a passenger.

Alarmed, Woodward asked Sweeney where the plane was. "I see water and buildings," she said. Then she cried, "Oh, my God! Oh, my God!" Suddenly, the phone went dead.

Within hours, Woodward and millions of other Americans learned the awful truth about Flight 11. The water Sweeney had seen was New York Harbor. The buildings were in Manhattan. At 8:45 A.M., Flight 11 smashed into the 110-story North Tower of the World Trade Center (WTC). The plane crashed into the tower at about the 90th floor.

The impact of the crash killed everyone on board and ignited the plane's 20,000 gallons (75,708 liters) of jet fuel. The WTC had turned into an inferno. Temperatures reached more than 2,000 degrees Fahrenheit (1,093 degrees Celsius). The building's structural steel columns began to melt like plastic.

Just after 9 A.M., another plane smashed into the WTC's South Tower at about the 60th story. It was United Airlines Flight 175. All 65 people on board died instantly.

At 9:30 A.M., U.S. President George W. Bush addressed the nation. He said that the United States had suffered a terrorist attack. At 9:43 A.M., American Airlines Flight 77, with 64 people on board, crashed into the Pentagon near Washington, D.C. The impact sent a fireball of debris flying into the lower floors of the five-story building.

Meanwhile in New York, the WTC towers continued to burn. The searing heat ravaged the steel structures. At 10:05 A.M., the South Tower collapsed. At 10:28 A.M., the North Tower also collapsed. The twin towers had taken several years to build. They took just seconds to collapse.

Across the nation, Americans watched and listened in horror. Televisions, radios, and the Internet delivered continuous coverage of the unthinkable events taking place. When people wondered if it could get any worse, news reporters announced that yet another plane had crashed. United Flight 93 had crashed in rural Pennsylvania. Officials thought that plane also had been hijacked. They guessed its target had been the White House, the U.S. Capitol, or Camp David.

Fortunately, Flight 93 never reached a target on the ground. Yet the 45 people on board were dead in the smoking crater the crash left behind.

The United States government began piecing together this terrorist attack. Everything led to one man living in a cave thousands of miles away in Afghanistan. He would soon be known as the most wanted terrorist in U.S. history: Osama bin Laden.

Pentagon Attacked

A military helicopter drops off rescue workers near the damaged Pentagon in Washington, D.C.

Who Is Osama bin Laden?

OSAMA BIN LADEN IS A MUSLIM, A FOLLOWER of the religion of Islam. Islam has about 1.2 billion followers worldwide. Osama bin Laden, however, is a Muslim fundamentalist, which means he follows a very strict interpretation (or reading) of the Koran, which is the holy book of Islam. Bin Laden believes there is only one, true way to be a good Muslim. He thinks it's okay to hurt or kill anyone who doesn't follow his reading of the Koran.

Most Muslims don't agree with bin Laden's interpretation of the Koran. Most believe he uses religion as an excuse for murdering people. He does not represent the vast majority of Muslims who live out their lives in peace according to their faith.

Osama bin Laden is a very rich man. He uses his money, which he inherited from his family, to support worldwide terrorism. His financial backing aides the organization and training of a growing terrorist network. He has been linked to many terrorist attacks against the United States and its allies.

Bin Laden's terrorist network operates in about 35 countries. Most of the Muslims in these countries are extremely poor. Many have been at war for years. Bin Laden brings a message of unity and salvation against a common enemy to these people. His followers rally to his cause as he buys them guns, military training, and food.

Osama bin Laden

Osama bin Laden at a secret location inside Afghanistan praising the September 11 terrorist attack on the United States.

Osama bin Laden communicates with his terrorist network by releasing religious rulings, called fatwas. The fatwas urge Muslims to declare war on the United States and Israel. He praises the killing of American civilians and military personnel in the name of Allah (the name for God in Islam). Islam is traditionally peaceful, loving, and sacred. But bin Laden has organized groups of discouraged Muslims to turn to violence and hatred as a means of preserving their culture.

The United States believes that bin Laden was behind the 1993 World Trade Center bombing. He was also named in the terrorist attacks of two U.S. embassies in Nairobi, Kenya, and Dar es Salaam, Tanzania, in 1998; the foiled millennium bombing plot in 1999; and the suicide mission on the guided missile destroyer USS *Cole* in October 2000. Many American civilians and military personnel were killed and injured in these attacks. In 1999, the Federal Bureau of Investigation (FBI) added bin Laden to its 10 Most Wanted list.

Today, bin Laden is the prime suspect in the September 11, 2001, attacks on the World Trade Center and the Pentagon. President George W. Bush has vowed to use all necessary resources to find and punish Osama bin Laden.

Pilgrims at Mecca

Thousands of Muslim pilgrims perform dawn prayers inside the Grand Mosque, Islam's holiest shrine, in Mecca, Saudi Arabia.

A Privileged Life

OSAMA BIN LADEN WAS BORN IN 1957, IN Jeddah, Saudi Arabia. He is the 17th of 52 children born to Muhammad Awad bin Laden. Osama's mother was one of Muhammad Awad bin Laden's several wives. Bin Laden's father died in 1967, leaving an estate of approximately $5 billion to his children. Osama bin Laden inherited millions of dollars after his father's death.

Osama bin Laden's father was a self-made billionaire. He founded the Bin Laden Group, a construction company that was very involved with Saudi government contracts. Osama learned the family business by working on construction projects during school holidays. He was a quiet and ordinary boy. During his teen years, he worked on the restoration sites at Mecca and Medina, the holy cities of Islam. It was at this time that he became very interested in the Islamic religion.

After bin Laden graduated from college, he went to work full time for the Bin Laden Group. He learned about government, finance, and construction. He also learned about building roads, moving equipment, engineering construction, negotiating contracts, and managing workforces. This knowledge helped him as he changed from an aristocrat to a revolutionary.

Lashing Out

Osama bin Laden criticizes the United States during a press conference in a secret location in Afghanistan.

To those who follow him, Osama bin Laden is a modest, shy, and reclusive man. He lives in caves, mud huts, or bunkers. He eats gritty bread with the rest of his army. Bin Laden has three wives and 15 children who live with him as he moves from one secret place to another every three or four days. As of May 2002, his whereabouts are unknown. Some guess he is hiding in the rugged wilderness areas along the border of Afghanistan and Pakistan. Since the attacks of September 11, 2001, the U.S. is determined to bring him to justice.

Show of Support

Demonstrators, some of them armed, show support for bin Laden at a rally in Pakistan.

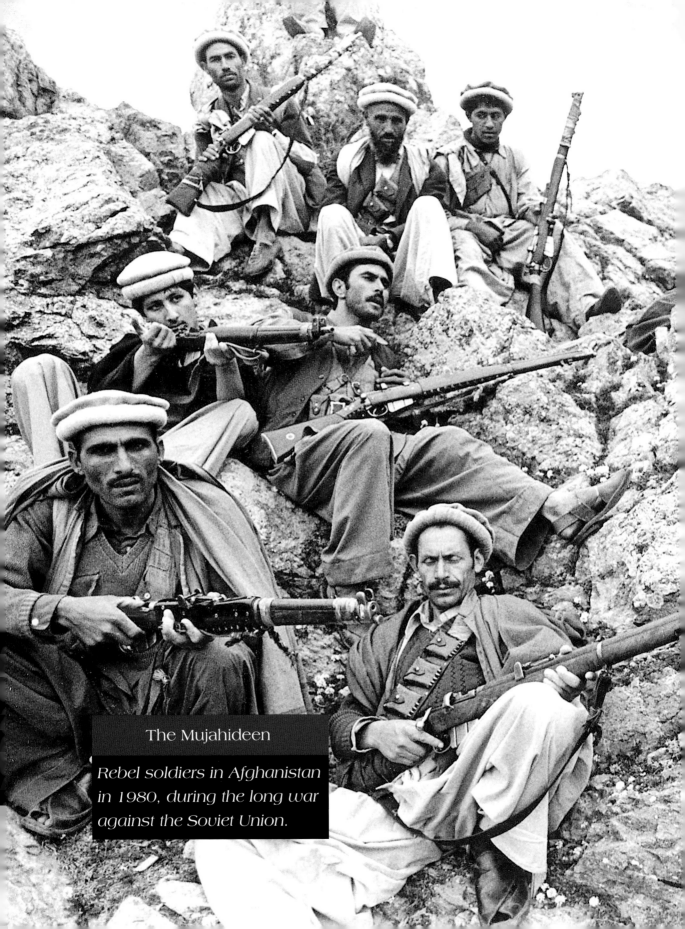

The Mujahideen

Rebel soldiers in Afghanistan in 1980, during the long war against the Soviet Union.

Rise To Power

O SAMA BIN LADEN BEGAN HIS MILITARY career when he went to fight in Afghanistan in 1979. During that year, the Soviet Union sent troops into Afghanistan to support the country's new Communist government. This attack on fellow Arabs disturbed bin Laden so much that he helped organize and train an army of thousands of Muslim volunteers, many of them Arabs from other countries, to fight the Soviets in Afghanistan. During the 10-year war, bin Laden became known as a militant not afraid to take on the world in his quest for Islamic unity.

The Afghan rebels received some financial and military supplies from the United States during this time. The U.S. wanted to foil the Soviets and stop the spread of communism. (The United States says no direct aid was given to bin Laden, however.)

The Afghan War ended when the Soviets left the country in 1989. Afterwards, bin Laden returned home to Saudi Arabia. He was angry with his homeland for allowing United States troops to be stationed there. He felt U.S. soldiers should not be allowed on holy Muslim land. Bin Laden wrote many letters and spoke out against the government, calling for its overthrow. Saudi Arabia stripped him of his citizenship and froze his bank accounts. Bin Laden soon relocated his fortune and moved to Sudan.

In 1996, the United States pressured Sudan to exile bin Laden or face political sanctions. Bin Laden was forced to return to Afghanistan, where he was welcomed as a champion of the Islamic Front. Bin Laden soon began building training camps and developing a terrorist alliance. He built a complex network of terrorists with members in more than 35 countries.

Bin Laden's dislike for the United States turned to hatred because Saudi Arabia and Sudan were now on the side of the Western superpower. He felt that the United States, a non-Muslim "infidel" country, had invaded Muslim holy lands. He decided to fight the U.S. with terror.

Bin Laden's network is responsible for many terrorist attacks around the world. U.S. and other foreign intelligence agencies link his influence to the 1993 bombing of the World Trade Center; a blast at the Egyptian Embassy in Pakistan; the murder of German tourists in Egypt; assassination plots against President Clinton, the pope, and the president of Egypt; and a scheme to blow up 12 American airliners over the Pacific Ocean.

Bin Laden's terrorist attacks share many of the same traits. A select core of trained leaders directs each attack. Only they know all the details. These leaders secretly plan and plot the attacks by coded message. Many of the plots have been foiled by Western intelligence efforts. Sadly, many more have been carried out with murderous zeal.

Osama bin Laden typically denies his involvement with any terrorist attacks, although he praises the efforts of those who have caused death and destruction to American targets.

WTC Bombing

The crater in an underground parking garage from the World Trade Center explosion in 1993. The blast left five people dead and several hundred injured.

The Prime Suspect

Osama bin Laden was shunned by his family in 1994.

Family Outcast

OSAMA BIN LADEN IS A MYSTERIOUS superterrorist. During the 1990s, bin Laden operated from hideouts in Afghanistan. He uses his own money and knowledge of business and technology to prepare terrorists to strike American targets. Bin Laden flies in his own private jet to Iran, Switzerland, the Philippines, and beyond. He controls millions of dollars in secret bank accounts to pay for his terrorist plots.

Many believe bin Laden used his money to help the Taliban take over Afghanistan after the Soviets left. He invented new ways of financing extremist movements by forming and funding his own terrorist network. He funnels money through organizations such as the Foundation for Islamic Salvation in the United States, Europe, and the Middle East to promote terrorist causes around the world.

The bin Laden family disowned Osama in 1994. They continue to deny any connection with him, his anti-American organization, or his fanatical religious beliefs. Bin Laden's terrorist attacks around the world are shocking and embarrassing to a family that is otherwise known to be generous, kind, and peaceful.

Some bin Laden family members live in the United States. They have spent some of their money in American businesses and schools. One bin Laden family member donated $1 million to Harvard University's Schools of Law and Design in order to bring understanding between the Western and Islamic worlds. Another bin Laden family member owns several luxury condominiums in Boston.

Former Presidents Jimmy Carter and George H. W. Bush both consulted with bin Laden family members with questions about economics and politics. Both presidents respected the financial success and political influence that this family had established as one of the world's richest companies. These relationships helped build a solid and trustworthy alliance between the United States and Saudi Arabia. But these relationships infuriated Osama bin Laden and further fueled his hatred for the United States.

After the attacks of September 11, several members of the bin Laden family who lived in the U.S. boarded a private plane and left the country. They left for their own protection, even though they denounced their brother for his terrorist acts.

In Hiding

Osama bin Laden makes a videotaped statement at a secret location in Afghanistan.

Armed and Dangerous

Osama bin Laden holds a Russian-made Kalashnikov rifle in 1998.

Why He Hates America

OSAMA BIN LADEN BELIEVES THE KORAN, the Islamic holy book, forbids Western countries from having a presence in Arab nations. His personal war against the United States began when Western troops were stationed in Saudi Arabia, the heartland of Islam, following Iraq's invasion of Kuwait in 1990. He was enraged that his homeland, Saudi Arabia, allowed this Western occupation during the Gulf War. The Saudi government denounced bin Laden for his violent objections. He was stripped of his Saudi citizenship for his actions.

Bin Laden also believes the West, especially the United States, has humiliated Arab nations by supporting Israel in the conflict with Palestine. He says the U.S. government has committed criminal acts. Bin Laden blames the suffering of the Palestinians on the United States.

Bin Laden and his Muslim extremist groups fear a U.S. conspiracy will destroy traditional Islamic culture and values. He believes America has the worst value system in the world. He thinks that democracy and our free society make us materialistic, with a sick desire for possessions instead of spiritual enlightenment. He believes the only way to create a pure Islamic state is to wage jihad, or holy war, against the U.S. and its allies and drive their forces out of Muslim lands.

Bin Laden issues fatwas (Islamic statements often calling for death to the enemies of Islam), as a way to rally his fanatic terrorist groups. Mainly, he asks his followers to kill Americans. Members of his network are not afraid to die fighting the enemy.

After numerous attacks, bin Laden was placed on the FBI's 10 Most Wanted list in 1999. There is a reward of up to $25 million for his capture. After the September 11 attack on America, a German millionaire also offered $10 million for information leading to the arrest and conviction of Osama bin Laden.

Blind Hatred

Supporters of Osama bin Laden burn a U.S. flag during a protest in Jakarta, Indonesia.

Al-Qaeda

DURING THE 1980s, THE UNITED STATES, Saudi Arabia, and other countries supported Afghan resistance troops called mujahideen. These "holy warriors" fought the Soviet invasion. Bin Laden left his comfortable life and went to Afghanistan to fight the Soviets alongside the mujahideen. He used his money and connections to build and strengthen the Afghan army by providing training, additional troops, and military supplies. He became a leader and hero in the 10-year battle.

Bin Laden's deep religious beliefs fueled his hatred of Western culture and values. During the Afghan War, he gained recognition and respect from other militants.

After the war ended, the mujahideen remained loyal to bin Laden and became the core members of al-Qaeda ("the base"). Al-Qaeda is a terrorist organization controlled by bin Laden that operates in many countries. This international network of radical groups and individuals is responsible for numerous deadly attacks against Western targets.

Al-Qaeda's goal is to overthrow all corrupt Muslim governments, drive Western influence from those countries, and become one state uniting all Muslims. The terrorist network has grown a lot since the bombings of the United States embassies. Global spy agencies have kept a close watch on many of the members. Today, al-Qaeda has terrorist members in the Middle East, Asia, Africa, Europe, plus North and South America.

Osama bin Laden uses his fortune to run terrorist training camps in Sudan, the Philippines, and Afghanistan. In these camps, militants prepare to fight alongside Muslim fundamentalists around the world. Bin Laden also provides money to other groups that want the destruction of the United States. Bin Laden considers the U.S. to be the chief obstacle standing in the way of a united Muslim society.

Terrorist Network

Osama bin Laden in Afghanistan. On the far left is one of bin Laden's top lieutenants, Egyptian Ayman al-Zawahri.

The Taliban

A Taliban soldier wraps his turban while on patrol in Afghanistan.

The Taliban

AFGHANISTAN IS A REMOTE, MOUNTAINOUS, landlocked country in between Iran, Pakistan, Turkmenistan, Tajikistan, Uzbekistan, and China. About 26 million people live there. Most of them are farmers. Most Afghans are Muslims. They are very patriotic and loyal to their country and religion.

Afghanistan is a country that has been at war for over 300 years, either with its enemies or among its own people. When the Soviets invaded Afghanistan in 1979, the United States, Saudi Arabia, and Pakistan gave money and weapons to fight the Communists. The Afghan Jihad grew stronger with this support. The Soviets finally left the country in 1989.

Osama bin Laden came to Afghanistan to fight the Soviets in order to preserve the Islamic cause. The war changed him mentally and spiritually. He became more committed to his religious beliefs but more revolutionary in his political beliefs. Bin Laden became a hero to many Afghans even after he went back to Saudi Arabia.

After bin Laden was expelled, first by Saudi Arabia in 1991, then by Sudan in 1996, Afghanistan offered him asylum. When he returned to Afghanistan, most of the country was under the control of the Taliban, an Islamic fundamentalist group. The Taliban has very strict rules that say how the Afghan people should live their lives. These rules are based on how the Taliban interprets the holy Koran.

Civil war following the Soviet exit from Afghanistan led to the rise of the Taliban movement. The Taliban, former Islamic seminary students, seized control of most of the country by 1996.

Despite its harsh Islamic practices, the Taliban brought law and order to a country torn by decades of war. The Taliban controlled all but the far north of the country. The Northern Alliance, a rebel band of fighters opposed to the Taliban, controlled this small section. In 2001, the Taliban assassinated the leader of the resistance in the north, Ahmed Shah Masood. By mid-November 2001, the Alliance struck back, capturing nearly 50 percent of the country with the help of U.S. air support.

The ruler of the Taliban, Mullah Mohammed Omar, imposes the strictest of Islamic law on the people of Afghanistan. He has forbidden music, television, movies, and most entertainment. Converting to a religion other than Islam is a crime punished by

death. Women are treated poorly. They are not allowed to work or go to school beyond grade school and must be covered from head to toe when outside of their homes. They have access to very limited medical treatment.

Osama bin Laden gave the Taliban money to boost its military when he returned to Afghanistan. He funded the training of Muslim terrorists from all over the world. The Taliban welcomed organizations such as al-Qaeda into Afghanistan and harbored international terrorists who threatened Western security.

World leaders and the United Nations do not recognize the Taliban. Afghanistan's former president, Burhanuddin Rabbani, holds the country's seat in the United Nations. The UN imposed sanctions against Afghanistan for harboring Osama bin Laden. These sanctions limit financial and economic aid to a desperate country under the militant rule of the Taliban.

U.S. Embassy Attacks

On August 7, 1998, the U.S. Embassy in Nairobi, Kenya, was struck by a terrorist's bomb. The explosion killed 213 people and injured thousands more. Osama bin Laden is believed to be responsible for the attack.

Targeting America

O SAMA BIN LADEN'S HATRED FOR THE United States is shown in his fatwas condemning Western values and occupation of Muslim holy lands. His threats became reality in 1993 with the first bombing of the World Trade Center. Six people were killed and hundreds were injured in the blast. Six known followers of Osama bin Laden were captured and tried for terrorism, conspiracy, and murder.

Bin Laden has also been connected with the attacks on a Yemeni hotel in 1992 that injured several tourists; a car bomb in Riyadh, Saudi Arabia, in 1995; a bomb in Dhahran, Saudi Arabia, in 1996 that killed 30 people; and an assassination attempt on Egyptian President Mubarak during a visit to Ethiopia in 1995.

Osama bin Laden and his group of terrorists continued to plan large-scale attacks. The bombing plot of the U.S. embassies in Nairobi, Kenya, and Dar es Salaam, Tanzania, in 1998 was uncovered by investigations following the attacks. It is believed that three men built both bombs. The Nairobi blast killed 213 people; 11 people were killed in Tanzania.

In December 1999, a terrorist linked to bin Laden's network was arrested after entering the U.S. from Canada at a border crossing north of Seattle, Washington.

Osama bin Laden is also the prime suspect in the bomb attack on the USS *Cole*, a guided missile destroyer, as it was fueling in the Yemeni port of Aden in October 2000. The blast killed 17 sailors, injured 39, and caused almost $100 million in damage to the ship.

By far the most horrendous plot blamed on bin Laden has been the September 11, 2001, attack on the World Trade Center and the Pentagon. Nineteen members of bin Laden's terrorist groups are linked to the attack.

USS *Cole* Attack

The USS Cole *after the terrorist attack in 2000 while in port in Yemen.*

Wanted Criminal

Osama bin Laden, in a photo from the FBI's Ten Most Wanted list.

Following the Money Trail

A U.S. Customs official at a raid in Seattle, WA, November 7, 2001, of a business suspected of having ties to Osama bin Laden's money network.

New Era Of Terrorism

I N THE PAST, MOST TERRORIST GROUPS GOT THE HELP of militant countries. Osama bin Laden's terrorist network reaches across national boundaries. Bin Laden's wealth, plus donations from supportive Muslims, buys training and weapons, making this an independent effort that relies on no state support and funding. It is estimated that bin Laden has no more than 2,000 troops at any one time. But they are well trained, well funded, and not afraid to die in order to inflict pain on their enemies. Technology and globalization makes their reach rapid and widespread.

Osama bin Laden's bunkers in Afghanistan are equipped with the latest computer equipment, fax machines, satellite-linked phones, and Internet access. Many of his orders are delivered over the Internet using special codes. United States spy agencies have intercepted some of these messages, but it takes special software and a lot of time to break the codes.

After the September 11, 2001, attack on America, bin Laden abandoned high-tech communication and resorted to low-tech methods to avoid detection. Intelligence agencies around the world are trying to track him. All communication methods are vulnerable in this age of technology. Bin Laden has reverted to personally delivering orders and receiving emissaries to avoid efforts to capture him.

FBI TEN MOST WANTED FUGITIVE

MURDER OF U.S. NATIONALS OUTSIDE THE UNITED STATES;
CONSPIRACY TO MURDER U.S. NATIONALS OUTSIDE THE UNITED STATES;
ATTACK ON A FEDERAL FACILITY RESULTING IN DEATH

USAMA BIN LADEN

Date of Photograph Unknown

Aliases: Usama Bin Muhammad Bin Ladin, Shaykh Usama Bin Ladin, the Prince, the Emir, Abu Abdallah, Mujahid Shaykh, Hajj, the Director

DESCRIPTION

Date of Birth:	1957	**Hair:**	Brown
Place of Birth:	Saudi Arabia	**Eyes:**	Brown
Height:	6' 4" to 6' 6"	**Complexion:**	Olive
Weight:	Approximately 160 pounds	**Sex:**	Male
Build:	Thin	**Nationality:**	Saudi Arabian
Occupation:	Unknown		

Remarks: Bin Laden is the leader of a terrorist organization known as Al-Qaeda, "The Base." He is left-handed and walks with a cane.

CAUTION

USAMA BIN LADEN IS WANTED IN CONNECTION WITH THE AUGUST 7, 1998, BOMBINGS OF THE UNITED STATES EMBASSIES IN DAR ES SALAAM, TANZANIA, AND NAIROBI, KENYA. THESE ATTACKS KILLED OVER 200 PEOPLE. IN ADDITION, BIN LADEN IS A SUSPECT IN OTHER TERRORIST ATTACKS THROUGHOUT THE WORLD.

CONSIDERED ARMED AND EXTREMELY DANGEROUS

IF YOU HAVE ANY INFORMATION CONCERNING THIS PERSON, PLEASE CONTACT YOUR LOCAL FBI OFFICE OR THE NEAREST U.S. EMBASSY OR CONSULATE.

REWARD

The Rewards For Justice Program, United States Department of State, is offering a reward of up to $5 million for information leading directly to the apprehension or conviction of Usama Bin Laden. An additional $2 million is being offered through a program developed and funded by the Airline Pilots Association and the Air Transport Association.

www.fbi.gov

June 1999
Poster Revised October 2001

Bringing bin Laden To Justice

FOR THE LAST DECADE, WESTERN FORCES have tracked Osama bin Laden. In 1998, President Bill Clinton ordered the bombing of terrorist camps in Afghanistan and Sudan. This was after the attacks on the two U.S. embassies in Africa. The U.S. attacks destroyed some camps, but failed to stop bin Laden.

After the September 11 attack on America, Secretary of State Colin Powell described bin Laden as no ordinary enemy. He said America had declared war on terrorism and promised to fight in the name of freedom.

The U.S. is asking all countries to help capture terrorists to preserve freedom and democracy. The West and its allies condemn terrorist attacks that kill and injure innocent people. The U.S. and global spy agencies are tracking the financial activity of bin Laden in an effort to freeze his money supplies. But Osama bin Laden has many followers, and he supports many terrorist groups. It will take more than bin Laden's elimination to end his dark legacy of terror.

Timeline

1957   Osama bin Laden born in Jeddah, Saudi Arabia. He is the 17th of 52 children born to Muhammad Awad bin Laden.

1967   Muhammad Awad bin Laden dies. Osama, at age 10, inherits millions from his father's estate.

1979   Osama bin Laden goes to Afghanistan to fight against the Soviets in the Afghan War.

1988   Formation of al-Qaeda.

1989   Soviet troops withdraw from Afghanistan. Osama bin Laden returns to Saudi Arabia.

1990   Beginning of the Persian Gulf War; the U.S. uses Saudi Arabian airfields in its attack on Iraq. Bin Laden is furious that U.S. occupies the Muslim holy lands.

1992   Osama bin Laden is suspected of involvement in a terrorist attack on a hotel in Arden, Yemen.

1993   Bombing of the World Trade Center in New York City. Six men who are suspected of terrorist association with Osama bin Laden are arrested.

1993   Bombing attack in Somalia.

1994   Osama bin Laden is expelled from Saudi Arabia for militant and dissident behavior against Saudi Arabia. His family disowns him.

1995   Bombing of U.S. military headquarters in Saudi Arabia.

1996   Osama bin Laden is exiled from the Sudan because of Western pressure. He takes refuge in Afghanistan. He considers it his religious duty to form the International Islamic Front for Jihad against Jews and Crusaders.

1996   Bombing of U.S. military barracks in Dhahran, Saudi Arabia.

1998   Bombing of U.S. embassies in Kenya and Tanzania 15 minutes apart.

1999   Police uncover millennium bombing plot. Osama bin Laden is placed on the FBI's 10 Most Wanted list with a $5 million reward for his capture.

2000   Suicide attack on USS *Cole* in Yemen.

2001   Terrorists fly two planes into the World Trade Center towers. Another plane crashes into the Pentagon. Another hijacked plane crashes in rural Pennsylvania.

        U.S. bombs targets in Afghanistan after ruling Taliban refuses to turn over bin Laden.

Where On The Web?

http://wral.com/sh/news/stories/nat-news-96144820010914-200910.html

A Middle East expert discusses Osama bin Laden's motives.

http://wral.com/sh/news/stories/archive/nat-news-archive-95739620010912-000926.html

A brief history of Osama bin Laden.

http://www.fas.org/irp/world/para/ladin.htm

Descriptions of Osama bin Laden's terrorist groups, including al-Qaeda and the International Islamic Front for Jihad Against Jews and Crusaders.

http://usembassy.state.gov/afghanistan/wwwhtr01.html

The U.S. government fact sheet on Osama bin Laden.

Glossary

Afghan War

The 10-year conflict between anticommunist Muslim guerillas and the Afghan Communist government aided by Soviet troops.

al-Qaeda

"The base," an organization of suspected terrorist groups under the control of Osama bin Laden.

Allah

The name for God in Islam.

alliance

A close association of nations or other groups formed to advance common interests or causes.

aristocrat

A member of a ruling class or nobility.

asylum

A place offering safety or protection.

capitalism

An economic system based on private ownership and reinvestment of profits gained in a free market.

conspiracy

A plot to carry out harmful or illegal acts.

democracy

Government by the people based on social equality and respect for the individual, which is ruled by elected representatives.

dissident

One who separates from the established religion.

extremist

One who resorts to measures beyond the norm and supports extreme practices or doctrines.

fatwa

"religious decree" or "ruling" in Arabic.

fundamentalists

A religious movement or point of view characterized by rigid adherence to specific principles and beliefs, and intolerance of other views or opposition.

holy land

An area of land considered sacred by a certain religious group.

jihad

"Holy War." To strive, struggle, and exert effort in Arabic.

Koran

The sacred text of Islam containing the revelations of Allah to Muhammad.

militant

A fighting, warring, or aggressive person or party. Terrorists are considered militants.

mujahideen

"Holy warriors." The name refers to Afghan fighters who fought against Soviet occupation of Afghanistan in the 1980s.

network

An intricate connection or system of people with mutual beliefs and political convictions.

perpetrator

One who commits an offense or crime.

Persian Gulf War

A war fought in 1991 in which a coalition of countries led by the United States destroyed much of the Iraqi military and drove its army out of Kuwait.

revolutionary

A militant in the struggle for revolution who supports subversive principles and actions.

Taliban

The militant Islamic group that rules Afghanistan according to strict Koran interpretation. The Taliban supports and protects Osama bin Laden.

Index